A Humble Mask on a Prideful Face

Daniel J. Fisher

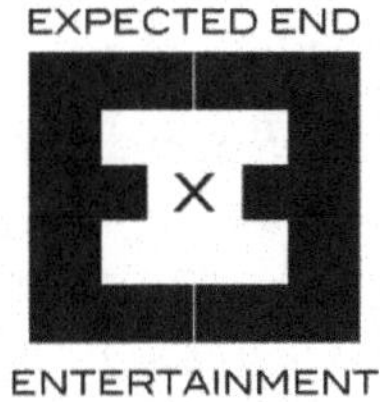

Atlanta, GA

Published by Expected End Entertainment/EX3 Books
ExpectedEndEntertainment@gmail.com
ISBN: 0988554526
ISBN-13: 978-0-9885545-2-8
Printed in the United States of America

DEDICATION

This book is dedicated to Linda Fisher, my beautiful bride of 11 years who taught me how to love God, love her and love myself.

ACKNOWLEDGEMENTS

Special thanks to the following:

- Paula Ponticel for all of your help, love and support.
- Crossroads Church for helping me to have a relationship with God.
- C. Nathaniel Brown for giving me a voice.

FOREWORD

I am no wiser than you. Any wisdom I possess, I have gained from making unwise decisions. I do not claim to know all of the answers, but 58 years on this earth has given me an opportunity to ask myself a lot of tough questions: What is really important in this life? Where does wholeness and joy come from? How do I find peace with the past, so I can live in the present?

In addition, marrying my wife, Linda, has done amazing things for my spiritual development. She not only gives me the love and accolades I desire but also the practical advice I need to continue growing. Accountability from people who care for you is important for growth. We all need an accountability partner. Entrusting our spiritual maturity with a loved one removes the defensive walls we naturally build to protect ourselves and helps us to find truth. In the gospel of John you can find one of the most profound messages about truth. John 8:32 states "Then you will know the truth and the truth shall set you free." This is my hope -- that this book will help you discover the freedom that only comes from knowing God and His truth.

CONTENTS

1	Introduction to Pride	1
2	Pride and Prayer	19
3	Pride and Church	35
4	Pride and Family	47
5	Pride and Friends	55
6	Pride and Work	65
7	Pride and God	73
8	Addendum	83
	About the Author	89

1

INTRODUCTION TO PRIDE

"I will break down your stubborn pride." Leviticus 26:19

There was a time in my life when my Christian walk was swiftly backsliding. I was a spiritual Benjamin Button, starting out as a grown man and regressing to a tiny baby. I had a spiritual reawakening in March 2014. I felt that God was guiding me to organize a Christian rock festival. As those plans quickly eroded, I took the event's demise personally. I learned that who I was serving in the beginning was not who I was serving at the end, and that was anything but humble.

I would love to say that I handled this failure well, but I didn't. Instead I fell into a depression. While planning the rock festival, I believed that I was in constant communication with God. Now, I could not hear His voice at all. When anyone whispers something in confidence, it is the expectation that we will lean in to hear what is shared. Even though God was whispering, I could not hear Him because my pride hindered my ability to lean.

One of the greatest quotes about pride can be found in C.J. Mahaney's book, Humility: True Greatness: "*Here is the great paradox: the proud man thinks he is humble, but the humble man thinks he is proud. The humble man sees his arrogance. He sees it clearly, and as a result he aggressively pursues a life of humility, but he doesn't think of himself as humble. The proud man is completely unaware of his pride. Of all men he is most convinced that he is humble*."

The planning of this concert forced me to ask myself this question: Did I gradually cease to be humble, or had I been prideful from the beginning? It all comes down to where our focus lies. We assume that if the outcome of our endeavors is for a greater good, then our intentions will be as well. This is what I refer to as the, "Who could possibly question" motive: If someone else benefits from our actions -- or better yet, if our actions glorify God -- then they *must* be humble!

We mislead ourselves when we think intent begins at the planning stage. It actually begins when we consider how others will see us and then believe they see us as a disappointment. This is why we are pushed to do well <u>and</u> to appear kind. A misconception about pride is that it primarily grows from the seeds of arrogance and vanity. Oftentimes, it comes from a place of insecurity and low self-esteem. As someone who has acted as the master of ceremonies on countless occasions, I cannot begin to tell you how many times I have uttered the phrase, "This next performer needs no introduction." The same can be said for pride. Introducing one to pride is like introducing one to breathing.

Young people are often told, “Watch what you’re doing!” But even as adults we need to heed this warning. We concentrate on the perception *of* others, rather than focus on the good we are doing *for* others. Think of it as “re-gifting” something broken or unattractive. Regardless of the beautiful paper and decorative bow, what’s inside is still unacceptable. Many times we are so consumed with how things appear that we overlook how they really are. As I planned and I prayed, I believed that the concert was not about me. But in sharing with others the details of my efforts, I realized I was unintentionally being prideful. The fact that I felt compelled to discuss my efforts made it about me. My goal was to honor God, but I still sought praise for myself.

How many of us are guilty of saying, “I always take great pride in my efforts to serve my church”? This is a self-absorbed statement. The fact that we use the words “*my church*” sends a clear message as to how we perceive things, and shows *our need for recognition* instead of *our need for God.*

As I write this, I struggle to understand something. How does a person humbly write a book about pride? In fact, how does a person humbly write a book at all? I ask myself this question in an effort to be more intentional. Being intentional is an action. Verbs are action words that are never stagnant. Verbs move. More often than not, I have been an adverb. Adverbs qualify a verb. I would discuss all of my plans with God, with friends at church and even with myself, about how I was going to be more motivated to serve. But I would never actually move.

We tend to see our pride in three ways: we *glance*; we *look*; or we *stare*. If we merely glance at our pride then we rarely address it. We know the pride is there, but it's quickly disregarded or forgotten. If we stare at our pride, we are so focused on the details that we never overcome it. We become so frozen by over-analyzing each of our options that we don't actually follow through on any of them. We have to really look at our pride and then become a verb and actually do something about it.

The planning of the rock concert was not the first time my pride became a distraction to serving God. Mark Twain said, "*write what you know*." Sadly, being prideful is a subject in which I am well versed. On the surface, anyone who meets me would not think I was prideful. If they do, they have never addressed it with me. Even the most combative person who is willing to take on any and all enemies will run and hide from the truth. As necessary as the truth may be, it is equally frightening because it forces us to own our every emotional and spiritual shortcoming.

I have learned an important lesson through the years. Just as we test the brakes on a new car, it is always good to test your spiritual brakes. It is always best to stop before you proceed and ask yourself, "What is my motivation?" The answer to this question doesn't always have to be *others*-based. In fact, motives that are completely *others*-based can be just as damaging as motives that are completely selfish. The first problem with being fully focused on others is that you become a car riding on fumes. Eventually you will run out of gas. My wife's favorite analogy comes from the instructions we receive from our flight attendant. We are told to place the oxygen mask on our own face before assisting others. A lack of self-preservation leads to spiritual and emotional suffocation. The second problem is that it gives us an opportunity to bask in a sense of, "I desperately need your approval" because I'm doing all this for you.

When this occurs, we define ourselves as victims. We desperately long to be right about anything -- so much so, we are willing to be *right* about always being *wrong*. Clearly, becoming a whiner or a complainer is a self-destructive by-product of that behavior. What is even more destructive is to become someone who "suffers in silence." Resentment builds because the other person does not instinctively recognize how we sacrifice to earn their approval. These emotional, spiritual and philosophical demons can be summed up as a perspective of not being good enough. If we do not see ourselves being good enough for people, then how can we see ourselves being good enough for God.

We all had dreams as children. When I was a kid, my dream was pretty simple --- I wanted to be a Boy Scout. I felt like I was a Cub Scout forever. I know this because nobody could make a pig out of a Clorox bottle as fast as I could. I wanted to move up the scouting food chain, so I practiced tying knots and reading the manual over and over. I went to my first Boy Scout meeting and the troop leader informed my dad that the scouts were probably not for me. I was a Boy Scout for literally two hours! I simply wasn't good enough.

So what is the answer to the question, "Am I good enough for God?" The quick answer is no: None of us is. The long answer starts in Romans 3:38 which states: *"So we are made right with God through faith and not by obeying the law."*

Everyone knows Jesus is perfect. Does that mean that to join Him in Heaven we must also be perfect? Obviously, that would be impossible! God gave us a solution in John 3:16: *"For this is how God loved the world: He gave His one and only Son, so that everyone who believes in Him will not perish but have eternal life."*

I am sure most of us are familiar with the saying, "The gift that keeps on giving." Because of His unfailing love for us, God constantly gives us His grace which is free and undeserved. We don't have to be perfect to go to church or pray to God. He doesn't ask us to move with perfection -- He just asks us to move.

I've done a lot of foolish things in my life, and at the ripe old age of 58 I'm probably not done doing foolish things. But God still loves me. I am still His child and when the day comes, He will welcome me home.

If we do not need to prove ourselves to God, then why do we feel the need to prove ourselves to others? This "need to prove" behavior is commonly referred to as codependence: a relationship in which someone is physically or psychologically addicted to a person or a relationship. Initially, it starts as a healthy connection. But in time can become harmful and lead us down a slippery slope toward becoming a martyr. Our submissive plea becomes an indignant barking of, "Look how much I sacrifice!"

To quote one of America's most incredible yet underestimated philosophers, Larry Fine from the Three Stooges, "Hey Moe… Hey Moe… I can't see… I got my eyes closed!" The reality is, nothing can be fixed in the dark. I believe that if we are completely honest with ourselves, we are all guilty of the same thing. We are notorious for closing our eyes so that we can invent our own version of the truth. Now keep in mind that pride can also be found in the light. Day does not suddenly become night and our perspective and responses to relationships are equally gradual. As we take this journey together we will discover that pride will be found hiding in the shadows of good intentions.

In my experience I have known two distinct types of pride. The '*knows*' and the '*nos*'. The '*knows*' live with the assumption that *everyone* will not only understand, but will also eventually agree with their thoughts, ideas and actions. The '*nos*' live with the assumption that *everyone* will disagree with their thoughts, ideas and actions and they are in a constant state of panic as they scramble to diffuse any negative responses. Although these two behavioral types are completely different, they both are propelled by the same desire: the ability to maintain control.

To understand where we are going, we must first examine where we have been, because that is where we first became either a '*know*' or a '*no*'. Our caregivers' expectations become our expectations. When their expectations for us are disappointment and failure, we become a negative, self-fulfilling prophesy. It is the child that is overexposed to neither the bright light of praise nor to the dark shadows of discouragement who grows to understand true balance.

Another immense difference between the '*knows*' and the '*nos*' is that the '*knows*' are unimpressed by what other people think whereas the '*nos*' are totally consumed by what other people think. This is why we hate to give up control -- not for the love of power but the fear of being misconstrued. Because we function in a constant state of redemption, we take every morsel of praise and hand it back in the form of an apology. We believe that a positive performance will automatically bring about a positive response, and we generally become despondent and give up if that does not occur.

As we progress, we will explore the root of this issue. But let us first explore the levels of pride through the parable of the seeds found in Matthew 13:3-9.

"Listen! A farmer went out to plant some seeds. As he scattered them across his field, some seeds fell on a footpath, and the birds came and ate them. Other seeds fell on shallow soil with underlying rock. The seeds sprouted quickly because the soil was shallow. But the plants soon wilted under the hot sun, and since they didn't have deep roots, they died. Other seeds fell among thorns that grew up and choked out the tender plants. Still other seeds fell on fertile soil, and they produced a crop that was thirty, sixty, and even a hundred times as much as had been planted! Anyone with ears to hear should listen and understand."

In this scripture we are reminded to ask ourselves, "Which seed am I?" The answer to that question can help determine your level of pride because pride is the most defiant form of independence. God has designed us to be dependent on Him. A life of self-reliance will limit our ability to succeed. It is God's desire for us to feel embraced but not imprisoned. He gave us free will. I would love to say that we usually choose wisely, but that's not always the case. Our spiritual growth is directly linked to our dependence on God. The more we depend on Him the more we grow.

SEED TO NEED CHART

SEED	NEED	DEPENDENCE
Seed eaten by birds	No Need for God	Fully on Self
Seed on shallow ground	Slight Need for God	Considerably on Self
Seed among thorns	Small Need for God	Fairly on Self
Seed on fertile soil	Complete Need for God	Fully on God

In all, there are over one hundred references to plants and trees in the Bible. It is a simple, yet profound, metaphor for life and growth.

Psalm 1:3 reads, "They are like trees planted along the riverbank, bearing fruit each season. Their leaves never wither, and they prosper in all they do."

Matthew 7:17-19 reads, "A good tree produces good fruit, and a bad tree produces bad fruit. A good tree can't produce bad fruit, and a bad tree can't produce good fruit. So every tree that does not produce good fruit is chopped down and thrown into the fire."

Pride, like any other sin, strangles the roots. Without the roots being fed, the plant will not grow. The deeper our roots are buried in pride, the faster our faith will die.

Americans love war. It is how we define our passion about something. We have declared war on everything that stands in the way of freedom. We've declared war on poverty, cancer, drugs and gangs. When we declare war it is with the belief that we will win. Even in Ephesians 6:17 Paul states: *"Be strong in the Lord and in his mighty power. Put on all of God's armor so that you will be able to stand firm against all strategies of the devil. For we are not fighting against flesh-and-blood enemies, but against evil rulers and authorities of the unseen world. Against mighty powers in this dark world, and against evil spirits in the heavenly places. Therefore, put on every piece of God's armor so you will be able to resist the enemy in the time of evil. Then after the battle you will still be standing firm. Stand your ground, putting on the belt of truth and the body armor of God's righteousness. For shoes, put on the peace that comes from the Good News so that you will be fully prepared. In addition to all of these, hold up the shield of faith to stop the fiery arrows of the devil. Put on salvation as your helmet, and take the sword of the Spirit, which is the word of God."*

If we were to declare war on pride then community would be our sword. Being in community battles pride in many ways. It forces us to trust that someone else can help us succeed at something we would prefer to do alone. It teaches us how to accept not only the help of others but their ideas as well. It also keeps us in check because ours is no longer the only ego in the room. Most importantly, it teaches us that we can never flourish in isolation. To imply that we are in combat may seem unnecessarily intense. Pride impacts every facet of our daily lives, and requires intense retaliation. True humility does not come naturally. It is hard. It takes a lot of strength and stamina to give all control to God.

We all have our one "thing." Our "thing" is any sin, desire or behavior we are too proud to hand over to God. It is so easy to have an "*I got this*" moment -- that moment when we delude ourselves into believing that we can resolve a problem on our own. When we do this, we create an unhealthy imbalance by inflating our abilities and deflating His. This proves that we long for the kind of freedom that can only be obtained from having a full relationship with our Heavenly Father. It is still not enough incentive to relinquish control. One of the greatest misconceptions is, "*God never gives us more than we can handle.*" Of course He does because if He didn't we would continue to live the lie that we don't need Him or others.

I would like to share my analogy of the three mirrors.

The first is a rear-view mirror which reminds us where we've been. There is a problem with living life looking in a rear view mirror. It simply becomes a reflection of who we were and not who we are. The second is a makeup mirror which is designed to help cover our imperfections. There is also a problem with living life looking in a makeup mirror. It only reflects a small portion of who we are and keeps the rest hidden. The third and best mirror is a full-length mirror because it is a reflection of all of us, and the more we move toward it, the more clearly we see our reflection. So which mirror are you using today?

Please do not feel that any of your answers will be incorrect. I assure you, even as I share my feelings and experiences, I change my answers. Honesty is like the sail on a ship. It steers us through the winds of change because an individual's truth is directly linked to that person's growth and circumstance. If our sense of what is true is not changing, then we have stopped asking questions. There is nothing more debilitating to our spiritual growth than assuming that we've learned enough. The problem with earthly progress is that it is horizontal. It is coming from the same space we are currently occupying, so there is no growth. Therefore strength and wisdom only come from a vertical source ---- God.

Please keep in mind this is not a self-help book. It cannot fix you. True healing can only be achieved with the strength and insight given by God. The problem with most books of that nature is that they tell us that the ability to change comes from within us -- and that is a lie. Instead of looking at our flaws and shortcomings as an albatross around our necks, look at them as tools in a toolbox. Use them to assemble and repair, a skill our Heavenly Father sent Jesus to teach us.

These are things I have not learned from my successes, but from my failures. It is through the setbacks that we learn to rely on God and, with each submission we become more and more humble. This entire process commences with knowing where we end and He begins. My desire is to remind both you and me that we cannot change what we will not acknowledge and that real power comes from God. I believe any journey involving change begins with one basic request to God: "Dear Lord, I no longer want to be what I've become. Show me the next step to transition into what you want me to become."

Before moving to the next chapter, I would like to share a personal hurdle that I recently experienced. Every summer, I dee-jay for the youth ministry at our church, and this summer I allowed the youth to help unpack my car.

Although both adults and youth have offered their assistance in the past, I always declined, saying, "I'm fine." I never let anyone help me when I unload and set up my equipment. I would allude that I am a perfectionist and prefer to do things myself. This trend actually comes from feelings of inadequacy and not being worthy of anyone's help. Whether pride is something we unwillingly project or intentionally execute, it is still an obstacle in our spiritual journey.

"I don't have this," or "Thank you, I could use some help," are sentences we fear will make us weak. But in fact they will make us strong. If we are unwilling to share the burden of our task, then how can we share the joy of our success? Joy is never meant to be cherished alone. As I acknowledge pride in my life and how it isn't just for the vain, I have discovered I certainly can keep a secret. In fact, I am so proficient at it that I kept my prideful behavior a secret not only from others, but also from myself. Hopefully we will learn to be honest about ourselves together.

Pride is the mask of one's own faults. **Jewish proverb**

2

PRIDE AND PRAYER

***Then if my people who are called by my name will humble themselves and pray and seek my face and turn from their wicked ways, I will hear from heaven and will forgive their sins and restore their land.* 2 Chronicles 7:14**

I do not believe that pride begins with one single event. Pride is not environmental. We usually do not become prideful based on circumstance, but instead, we address each circumstance based on our prideful nature. This is how an isolated circumstance becomes a pattern. In other words, pride is internal so we tend to weave it into the fabric of everything we do. If pride lightly touches aspects of our lives like a sprinkle of rain, then pride saturates our prayer life like a torrential downpour. No one can honestly say that they never engage in prideful prayer.

Prideful prayer is basically prayer with a self-serving agenda. Generally there are two types of prayers. Prayers of '*want*' and prayers of '*need*'. Prayers that come from a place of *want* are typically self-seeking. Prayers that come from a place of *need* are often more desperate in nature. For example, I may pray for the healing of a sick child and my prayer is from a place of 'want'. However, if it's *my* child my prayer comes from a place of 'need' because the outcome directly impacts my life. I have found during my prayers of want I often pray the request but don't take the time to listen for God's answer. As a result, my prayer time became a monologue rather than a dialogue.

To understand the magnitude of my '*want'* prayer, you need to know two things about me. First, it has always been my desire to have a vocation that would allow me to use my creativity. Second, I spent most of my life admiring people in the entertainment world thinking "if only I could be famous like them". I would often remind myself if I couldn't become a boy scout, how could I ever become famous. So I packed away my shoebox of ideas and dreams and settled for an ordinary life.

One afternoon that all changed. I was meeting my wife Linda for lunch at a local restaurant. As I impatiently waited, I happened to run into an old acquaintance having breakfast with a man we will call Tom. I quickly learned Tom had a local studio and aspired to produce television programs. Since I aspired to create television programs, this rekindled my dream. I believed Tom was sent by God to partner in that dream. I quickly unpacked my shoebox filled with TV show ideas and my prayers of *want* began. I truly believed God knew the desires of my heart, and therefore had to be the driving force behind these events.

As a result we went to work. I shared multiple ideas and finally agreed upon an animated sitcom. We worked for months diligently developing the characters and the pilot. Having the opportunity to both write and illustrate the pilot was so exhilarating I had no other choice but to believe it was ordained by God.

This is a perfect example of how splintered my view of God was. I assumed if it made me happy then it must be God's will. One of the most prideful foundations in anyone's prayer life is the assumption that God wants for us the same things we want for us.

It would be safe to assume that I bought into Tom's dream of producing a TV show… hook, line and sinker. After years of investing in the dream I discovered he had swindled many of his business associates and was padlocked out of the studio.

I now wonder if there were signs form the beginning that would have revealed Tom's true character. The answer is yes. Unfortunately dreams and truth don't always share the same space. Therefore, I chose to dream…

My initial response when the dream fell apart was to ask where was God and why didn't He answer my prayer of want? After all, I was a nice guy. I served at my church. In fact, I was on a mission trip when I received the phone call informing me I had been betrayed. My heart was broken as I mourned the death of my dream.

I have learned there are three different voices in our head. First we have our own voice, which has human limitations—It's clouded. Second we have God's voice, which is pure and desires the best for us --- It restores. Finally we have the enemy's voice, which is dark and wants the worst for us --- It destroys. What further complicates this process is our inability to discern because all three voices sound the same.

But as revealed in James 4:2-3: *"Yet you don't have what you want because you don't ask God for it. And even when you ask, you don't get it because your motives are all wrong-you want only what gives you pleasure."* The truth is God did answer my prayer, and the answer was no. I had lost focus on the reality that I am loved and accepted by God--- the one who created the world. So why was I trying so hard to be loved and acceptance by the world He created? Often times we ignore God when He says no, because pride assures us the answer should be yes. Therefore, we feel neglected by God when we are really being protected by God.

My second example is based on a prayer of '*need'*. One morning I suddenly became ill with what I thought was a migraine. I proceeded to the PCP office and while I was sitting in the waiting room, I turned to my wife and whispered "I am dying". Now I realize men tend to exaggerate when not feeling well, but in my case, it was actually true. It only required a two-minute consultation with my doctor before I was rushed to the hospital with a diagnosis of meningitis.

There are two types of meningitis. Viral meningitis, which is a virus and not fatal. Bacterial meningitis, if not treated immediately, can be fatal. After initial testing including a spinal tap, I was diagnosed with bacterial meningitis. This struck fear in both of us. I have given my wife, Linda the nickname "Dr. Google" because of her zealous manner in which she researches medical conditions. She thinks she is a doctor, but she's not. She is a prayer warrior and immediately started making phone calls and rallying an army of other prayer warriors. I soon became a "medical head scratcher". After the initial diagnosis and several hours of testing and prayer, the doctors had no explanation as to why the diagnosis went from bacterial meningitis to viral meningitis--but we knew.

My intention of sharing this story is not to debate if present day miracles are real. My intention is to display the importance of community. My wife did not phone our church family based on a 'want' but rather a desperate 'need'. I believe it was the intervening prayers that saved my life. This proved that I was blessed in two ways. I had a church family that cared enough to pray for me, but most importantly I had a wife that recognized she could not do this alone. If solitude were God's plan for humanity then creation would have stopped with Adam. Anytime we choose to live in isolation from other believers, we are isolating ourselves from God.

My final example is a combination of both *'want' and 'need' prayers.* Before Linda, I was married to Vivian for 17 years. Vivian had a personality bigger than life. She told a good joke when you needed a laugh, and offered a shoulder when you needed compassion. As the years went by, Vivian's gradual weight gain led to the diagnosis of diabetes. Diabetes led to neuropathy, and neuropathy led to severe pain.

Over time, Vivian's health deteriorated beyond the point of resolve and she chose to have gastric bypass surgery. Sadly, Vivian was only given one full day of hope, and then we lost her. On the day that she died I did not believe that Jesus cared and he certainly wasn't my friend. One of Jesus greatest miracles involved two sisters praying a desperate prayer of 'need' just like me. The story of

Lazarus can be found in John 11:1-44:

A man named Lazarus was sick. He lived in Bethany with his sisters, Mary and Martha. This is the Mary who later poured the expensive perfume on the Lord's feet and wiped them with her hair. Her brother, Lazarus, was sick. So the two sisters sent a message to Jesus telling him, "Lord, your dear friend is very sick."

But when Jesus heard about it he said, "Lazarus's sickness will not end in death. No, it happened for the glory of God so that the Son of God will receive glory from this." So although Jesus loved Martha, Mary, and Lazarus, He stayed where He was for the next two days. Finally, he said to his disciples,

"Let's go back to Judea." But his disciples objected.

"Rabbi," they said, "only a few days ago the people in Judea were trying to stone you. Are you going there again?" Jesus replied,

"There are twelve hours of daylight every day. During the day people can walk safely. They can see because they have the light of this world. But at night there is danger of stumbling because they have no light." Then He said, "Our friend Lazarus has fallen asleep, but now I will go and wake him up." The disciples said,

"Lord, if he is sleeping, he will soon get better!" They thought Jesus meant Lazarus was simply sleeping, but Jesus meant Lazarus had died. So he told them plainly,

"Lazarus is dead. And for your sakes, I'm glad I wasn't there, for now you will really believe. Come, let's go see him."

Thomas, nicknamed the Twin, said to his fellow disciples,

"Let's go, too—and die with Jesus."

When Jesus arrived at Bethany, he was told that Lazarus had already been in his grave for four days. Bethany was only a few miles down the road from Jerusalem, and many of the people had come to console Martha and Mary in their loss. When Martha got word that Jesus was coming, she went to meet him. But Mary stayed in the house.

Martha said to Jesus,

"Lord, if only you had been here, my brother would not have died. But even now I know that God will give you whatever you ask." Jesus told her,

"Your brother will rise again."

"Yes," Martha said, "he will rise when everyone else rises, at the last day."

Jesus told her,

"I am the resurrection and the life. Anyone who believes in me will live, even after dying. Everyone who lives in me

and believes in me will never ever die. Do you believe this, Martha?"

"Yes, Lord," she told him. "I have always believed you are the Messiah, the Son of God, the one who has come into the world from God." Then she returned to Mary. She called Mary aside from the mourners and told her, "The Teacher is here and wants to see you." So Mary immediately went to him. Jesus had stayed outside the village, at the place where Martha met him. When the people who were at the house consoling Mary saw her leave so hastily, they assumed she was going to Lazarus's grave to weep. So they followed her there. When Mary arrived and saw Jesus, she fell at his feet and said,

"Lord, if only you had been here, my brother would not have died." When Jesus saw her weeping and saw the other people wailing with her, a deep anger welled up within him, and he was deeply troubled.

"Where have you put him?" he asked them. They told him,

"Lord, come and see." Then Jesus wept. The people who were standing nearby said,

"See how much he loved him!" But some said,

"This man healed a blind man. Couldn't he have kept Lazarus from dying?" Jesus was still angry as he arrived at

the tomb, a cave with a stone rolled across its entrance.

"Roll the stone aside," Jesus told them. But Martha, the dead man's sister, protested,

"Lord, he has been dead for four days. The smell will be terrible." Jesus responded,

"Didn't I tell you that you would see God's glory if you believe?" So they rolled the stone aside. Then Jesus looked up to heaven and said, "Father, thank you for hearing me. You always hear me, but I said it out loud for the sake of all these people standing here, so that they will believe you sent me." Then Jesus shouted,

"Lazarus, come out!" And the dead man came out, his hands and feet bound in grave clothes, his face wrapped in a head cloth. Jesus told them,

"Unwrap him and let him go!"

There are times when we are so engrossed in the fact that Jesus is God that we overlook the fact that He was also human. This brings me to the shortest sentence in the Bible… "Jesus wept." If Jesus knew Lazarus was going to be raised from the dead, why did he weep? Jesus wept because He doesn't just stand back and watch us suffer, but He shares in our suffering.

After Vivian died I spent many nights crying myself to sleep. I now realize that when I wept, Jesus wept. During this time people would often say "I know how you're feeling". It was said with the best intentions, but the truth is that they didn't know how I was feeling. However, God knew because He sacrificed His only son to die on the cross, He knows pain and loss. There are very few emotions more humbling than sorrow. It is all consuming. It has no filter, no agenda. It is raw and honest.

Jesus never wastes a teachable moment. No life experience ends without an unexpected reward or an unforeseen lesson. I once read in Dear Abby, bereavement can be described as a ship leaving a port and taking people to a new home. The people standing on the dock cry tears of sorrow as the ship gets smaller and smaller. The people on the other dock cry tears of joy because the ship is bringing its passengers to a new home. Jesus is on both shores of the journey. He shares in the sorrow with those left behind and in the joy with those coming to spend eternity with Him.

Those were comforting and insightful words, but I was too broken and bitter to appreciate the sentiment. When Vivian was dying my prayers of 'need' that God would save her life were answered with a 'no'. So soon after her death my motivation shifted to prayers of 'want' simply because I could not stand to be alone.

For two and a half years, my world was consumed with a combination of resentment towards God and indifference toward others. I desired to share my life with someone, but ironically I continued to build a wall to keep others out.

In the various forms of pride one can immerse, isolation is the most dangerous. This kind of disconnect robs you of peace, joy and eliminates accountability in one fell swoop.

At the time I worked at a video store that also featured tanning beds. Although this work allowed many opportunities to meet women only one caught my attention. It was not her captivating smile or her gorgeous blue eyes that drew me in. It was her peaceful presence.

I am the first to admit my observational skills are lacking, but after she played the same Christian CD on our first four dates I could not help but notice a pattern. My suspicions were solidified when she asked me if I had faith. I replied with the safe and standard answer 'I am spiritual but not religious'. Any Christian will tell you, this is secret code for 'please do not tell me about your church and certainly don't invite me'.

Friday was my day off and soon became date night. I knew it would bring a lovely dinner, the company of a beautiful woman and the dreaded invitation to church. This went on for several weeks and so did my excuses. I hesitated to attend service with her because accepting her offer would illuminate my sense of rejection from God. Unlike Linda who knew God to be a source of peace, I only knew him to be the source of the bitterness that perpetuated my prideful nature.

Since most of my adult life was spent in a state of separation from God, everything I knew about believers I learned from unbelievers. Therefore, why would I choose to be in a room filled with people I believed to be closed-minded and judgmental?

I thought it was not possible for their love to fill the holes in my broken heart. For those unfamiliar with spackle, it is designed to fill the holes in a wall. God wanted to fill the holes in my heart and in my life, but God is not intrusive. To embrace his love we must first surrender our pride and recognize our need for him.

It is very common to have the things we perceive we want and ignore the things that we actually need. Even on those rare occasions we believe we have a firm grasp on what we need, our perception is blurred by our inability to see the full picture because as humans we gauge our success by worldly standards.

I eventually accepted the invitation to attend church with Linda. I am happy to say eleven years later I am still attending. God answered my prayers of ‘want’ by giving me a loving wife. God exceeded my expectations by answering my prayer of ‘need’. He used Linda to help me realize my true need was a relationship with Him.

Early in my relationship with God I would be the first to admit prayer did not come naturally. Prideful prayer is self- seeking, but authentic prayer is based on a *relationship* with God. Whether we are praying prayers of ‘want’ or praying prayers of ‘need’, Jesus gave us a guideline on how to pray, which is commonly known as the Lord’s Prayer found in Matthew 6: 9-13.

“Our Father Who art in heaven, Hallowed be Thy name.” Honor God and acknowledge His greatness.

“Thy kingdom come Thy will be done, On earth as it is in heaven.” Surrender your will to God’s will.

“Give us this day our daily bread.” Ask God for your needs and the needs of others. .

“And forgive us our debts, as we also have forgiven our debtors.” Ask God for forgiveness and offer forgiveness to others.

"And do not lead us into temptation, but deliver us from evil." Ask God for the grace to stand firm in the face of temptation.

"For Thine is the kingdom, and the power, and the glory, forever. Amen." Proclaim who God is and Exalt His name.

On many occasions I have allowed my pride to distract me from God. I've drifted away from God and even turned my back on God. But God is constant, He never moves, He is unchanging. I still do not always conduct my prayer life with the healthiest balance, but I can say that I possess a more grateful outlook on life. God listens to our prayers, but we have to be persistent. These experiences have taught me that sometimes His answer to my prayer is 'no' and sometimes His answer to my prayer is 'yes', but all the time God is all knowing, all loving and remains faithful.

A proud man is always looking down on things and people; and, of course, as long as you're looking down, you can't see something that's above you. **C. S. Lewis**

3

PRIDE AND CHURCH

In his pride the wicked does not seek him; in all his thoughts there is no room for God. Psalm 10:4

Nothing is more life changing than the realization the Creator of the Universe desires a relationship with you. I finally accepted Linda's invitation to church. It was at church I was able to reach beyond my pain and for the first time feel God's love. The parable of the prodigal son gave me hope and helped me realize that despite my poor choices, I was still loved by God. The parable of the prodigal son can be found in Luke 15:11-32:

"Jesus told them this story: "A man had two sons. The younger son told his father, 'I want my share of your estate now before you die.' So his father agreed to divide his wealth between his sons. "A few days later this younger son packed all his belongings and moved to a distant land, and there he wasted all his money in wild living. About the time his money ran out, a great famine swept over the land, and he began to starve. He persuaded a local farmer to hire him, and the man sent him into his fields to feed the pigs. The young man became so hungry that even the pods he was feeding the pigs looked good to him. But no one gave him anything.

"When he finally came to his senses, he said to himself," At home even the hired servants have food enough to spare, and here I am dying of hunger! I will go home to my father and say, "Father, I have sinned against both heaven and you, and I am no longer worthy of being called your son. Please take me on as a hired servant."

"So he returned home to his father. And while he was still a long way off, his father saw him coming. Filled with love and compassion, he ran to his son, embraced him, and kissed him. His son said to him, 'Father, I have sinned against both heaven and you, and I am no longer worthy of being called your son."

"But his father said to the servants, 'Quick! Bring the finest robe in the house and put it on him. Get a ring for his finger and sandals for his feet. And kill the calf we have been fattening. We must celebrate with a feast, for this son of mine was dead and has now returned to life. He was lost, but now he is found.' So the party began.

"Meanwhile, the older son was in the fields working. When he returned home, he heard music and dancing in the house, and he asked one of the servants what was going on. 'Your brother is back,' he was told, 'and your father has killed the fattened calf. We are celebrating because of his safe return.'

"The older brother was angry and wouldn't go in. His father came out and begged him, but he replied, 'All these years I've slaved for you and never once refused to do a single thing you told me to. And in all that time you never gave me even one young goat for a feast with my friends. Yet when this son of yours comes back after squandering your money on prostitutes, you celebrate by killing the fattened calf!

"His father said to him, 'Look, dear son, you have always stayed by me, and everything I have is yours. We had to celebrate this happy day. For your brother was dead and has come back to life! He was lost, but now he is found!'"

Just as the prodigal son returned to his father I returned to my Heavenly Father. The church was the first place to show me that despite my history, I was still welcomed. I have to admit that I loved attending church from day one. On the way home Linda asked me to share my thoughts about the service. I said, 'you have karaoke at your church'. Judging by the look on her face, I had obviously confused her but then I added, 'you put the words on the screen so everyone can sing along' – karaoke. This was a new concept to me, and I was very pleased because I love karaoke.

My first visit to Linda's church was very eye opening, because I was a stranger to the concept of 'come as you are'. I was raised Catholic and believed God was so powerful that all communication had to be conveyed through the priest. I was far too inadequate to speak to God on my own. My preconceived notion of church-goers was that they were well-dressed, well-behaved, questioned nothing, and most importantly nothing like me.

During my first visit I would like to say that I was most impressed by everyone's joy and compassion, but the truth is I was most impressed by the casual dress code. The people were warm, accepting and compassionate and through them I learned that God was too. Much to my surprise, I quickly discovered that God's house can also be a home. I learned that my past does not dictate my future. God taught me to stop apologizing for my past and begin using it as evidence of my transformed life. All this lead to a desire to share with others that there is another choice, another path, and God's grace was available to them--- just like me.

After attending for only a few months, the assistant pastor approached me about becoming more involved. Soon after, I became invested in the children's ministry. This ministry came naturally to me since I have always had a love for children. I was more than willing to serve with abandon, and it didn't hurt that serving came with a side order of 'feeling needed'.

Early on, I did not feel I was worthy of God's grace based on the condition of my heart ---- so I felt compelled to earn it from the sweat of my brow. The thought process was instilled in me by being raised Catholic and maintaining a relationship with God by worldly standards. Because of this I did not understand the concept of grace. God's grace can be defined as a "free and undeserved" gift. It was easier for me to disguise my pride by scurrying to serve and avoid facing God. Since I knew I fell short of man's expectations I believed I fell short of God's.

This is what I refer to as 'Check-the-Box-Christianity'. You have a to-do-list of all the things a good Christian 'supposedly' does but there is no authenticity in the actions. It is much like the husband that believes his level of obligation towards his family ends at bringing home a paycheck thereby exempting him from any emotional interaction. As a 'Check-the-Box Christian' I was able to feel good about myself <u>and</u> feel useful without actually having an intimate relationship with God.

Quickly, I grew into a serve-aholic. Which is someone whose pride prevents them from saying 'no' and they continue to say ‘yes’ for all the wrong reasons. You will never find a more diligent crew of laborers than people-pleasers on a divine mission. I came to this conclusion when I volunteered for the single mom’s oil change. I knew very little about the inner-workings of a car, and so my job was to stand behind the vehicle to let them know if the turn signals were working properly. Clearly, auto mechanics is not my spiritual gift. I was already using my spiritual gift serving in the children’s ministry-- so why wasn’t that enough?

The problem isn’t with serving, because spiritual growth becomes stagnate without serving. We must look at our intentions behind the serving. It was from serving with a prideful intent that I discovered my mask of humility. I finally realized it became less about people knowing God’s love and more about people knowing me. When presented with an opportunity to serve, every decision should start with a prayer for discernment.

God commissions each one of us. Jesus illustrates this in Matthew 28:16-20 known as--- The Great Commission:

...Jesus came and told his disciples, “I have been given all authority in heaven and on earth. Therefore, go and make disciples of all the nations, baptizing them in the name of the Father and the Son and the Holy Spirit. Teach

these new disciples to obey all the commands I have given you. And be sure of this: I am with you always, even to the end of the age."

Notice it doesn't say when you serve you are guaranteed to receive accolades. So we need to ask ourselves: Are we serving based on Jesus' commission or is it more about our condition? Ironically we find it easier to serve seeking worldly approval, rather than serving an Almighty God that has already given His approval. Anytime we attempt to fill the void in our lives with the 'created' rather than the 'Creator' we are relying on substitutes. Fulfillment derived from substitutes is both fleeting and temporary.

Intellectually, we know this to be true. Satan relies on convenience in his quest to distract us from God. Satan's lure of pleasure is instant and feeds into our sinful nature. Since pleasure precedes regret, we often choose instant gratification. One of the most prideful forms of instant gratification is serving with the only goal of receiving accolades. We put on our humble mask to imply we are serving based on God's truth, but in reality we put on our humble mask to keep our prideful intent a secret. The world would have us believe the lie that every good deed deserves a reward. When we serve without humility we deny ourselves the true joy of giving. Thankfully God isn't of this world, so serving Him comes with an eternal reward. We have to accept that we don't always have the luxury of seeing the fruits of our labors. Serving is similar to a relay race: one person starts then hands the baton to another who hands it to another. We are often just a cog in the wheel, and don't always get to cross the finish line.

Since we all fall short of the Glory of God, a horizontal focus toward man will always fall short. It is only when we have a vertical focus toward God that we can feel the joy of giving without a need for receiving praise. We can trust that he is in control of the outcome.

'What does trust have to do with pride in the church?' Everything! Our lack of trust began when we first became a '***no***'. If we reflect on our pride-filled battle to maintain control, much of that behavior would be linked to our inability to trust. Our inability to trust can be directly linked to a lack of validation during our early development.

Our pride comes from not trusting how others will respond to us or how others will perceive us. One of my favorite quotes about trust comes from holocaust survivor Corrie Ten Boom who said, *"Never be afraid to trust an unknown future to a known God."* As we all know, even

Jesus, the Son of God, was betrayed by one of his trusted disciples.

Hebrews 10:23 says:

"Without wavering, let's hold tightly

to the hope we say we have for God

can be trusted to keep his promise."

Even when people let us down, God can always be trusted.

Pride evolves from the erosion of our self-esteem over a period of time. Therefore, it would be foolish to believe that humility would be instantly achieved. I have found the following steps helpful in finding humility and rebuilding trust:

REFLECT	RESPONSE
Honesty • We can't change what we don't acknowledge	• Find an accountability partner with whom you can be completely honest and meet with regularly.
Prayer • Reflect on God's word	• Find a signature verse that speaks to you, to begin to see yourself as God sees you. Some examples are: Matthew 19:26 Ephesians 4:24 Philippians 4:7 Ephesians 2:8 Philippians 4:13 Jeremiah 29:11
Forgiveness • Forgiving doesn't mean condoning. • Forgiveness relinquishes the desire to get even and restores our ability to trust.	• Forgiveness isn't a feeling, it's a choice. • A process that requires patience. • To be successful you must relinquish all expectation of the outcome.
Restoration • God's transformation in our lives brings healing.	• Transformation begins by building a relationship with God by spending time with Him daily.

I have served, and worshiped alongside people who are just as imperfect as me. Since 'we' are the church, we will never attend a perfect church. Because the perfect church doesn't exist, we can stop looking--- because we serve and worship a perfect God. As I continue to grow in my faith, the voices from my past that told me I could do nothing have been replaced by a Heavenly voice that tells me I can do anything--- through Him. I once considered words such as 'surrender' and 'humility' words of weakness. Now I realize they are actually words of strength. Pride, just like any other demon, will always battle for our attention. God has never lost a battle.

Temper gets you into trouble. Pride keeps you there.
Unknown Source

4

PRIDE AND FAMILY

See what kind of love the Father has given to us, that we should be called children of God; and so we are…
I John 3:1

One word makes me cringe like no other -- Danny. I am 58 years old and my family still refers to me as Danny. I feel that it is said with a tone of nostalgic disapproval. This feeling isn't generated based on my family's disdain for me, but based on their love for boxes. Families tend to put us in boxes based on their memories of our behavior when we were children. Pride comes into play when we instinctively need to escape the box by changing our persona in their eyes.

Our world begins with our family. Our family members often believe that they know us better than anyone. But in truth they often know us the least. It is in the context of 'family' that the initiation process of becoming a ***'no'*** begins. Our families tend to mentally keep us confined to their image of us in the past. In their minds we are still the young children who deeply need their guidance. Ironically we strive to prove how much we have grown to the very people who are invested in us remaining the same.

Our actions change when we do not receive the responses we anticipate, even though the other individual had no idea we even had those expectations. So this lack of communication leads to disappointment, which leads to resentment and prideful inner dialogue as to how we are misunderstood or unappreciated.

I thoroughly excelled in school, unless of course you count grades, athletic ability or general popularity. Growing up I had one brother who excelled in academics, and one brother who excelled in sports. Then there was me who excelled in '*the arts*'

Every weekend I would write, direct, and star in a play. I would perform in my own back yard for a sold out audience. The key to having a sold out audience was the fact I used their five cent admission to feed them penny candy during the show. I obviously took greater pride in my ability to entertain than successfully managing my business.

My artistic abilities did nothing to impress my father who worked in a steel mill and served in World War II. In addition to my father's inability to fathom what made me tick, was his sarcasm, which at times was mean. One of his favorite comments was "You are a pimple on the ass of progress." Becoming a ***'no'*** doesn't come from one snide remark. Instead it comes from a series of snide remarks, followed by a self-loathing inner dialogue. It is often a long and tedious process involving years of self-doubt based on feelings of inadequacy.

Often just our words can be our greatest weapon when trying to hurt another. This is clearly illustrated in James 3:5-12: *"In the same way, the tongue is a small thing that makes grand speeches. But a tiny spark can set a great forest on fire...*

Our families have access to the words that can cause the most pain. Often these battles are not strategic or even intentional. Often when we feel threatened we tend to reach for words impulsively and give no thought to the damage they have on the individual on the receiving end. Any time words are used in this manner, the one on the receiving end becomes too defensive to see that at the core of the aggressor lies the same feelings of inadequacy found at the heart of a ***'no'***. Therefore, rather than our response being peaceful and grounded in truth, we continually try to prove our worth to disprove their inaccuracy. Sometimes pride causes us to work to break those patterns and attempts to disprove our family's concept of us. Ironically, our desire is for them to recognize our growth, but they desire us to recognize theirs. This struggle to be heard has the potential to become an underlying competition and that competition elevates our prideful nature.

A ***'no'*** will tell you that the best way to change our image is by doing something we can be proud of to validate our worth. We generally view accomplishments as 'receipts' as proof of our growth. Pride is a state of being that comes from either a place of fullness or emptiness and my pride grew from the latter.

As a ***'no'***, I lived in a state of "if only" - "if only" I were taller, "if only" I were smarter, "if only" I were more athletic-- then maybe others would accept me. The more fragmented my relationships were with others the more I focused on my weaknesses rather than my strengths. This is why we cannot say that we are too broken to be prideful. The truth is that the lure of the spotlight isn't only spawned by the assumption that we are too good, but also the presumption that we are not good enough.

We do not live in a black and white world. Nothing is completely good or bad. More often than not it is somewhere in between. Families are no different. Families can be an excellent source of love and support. Not even our family has the ability to take control of our lives. We would have to give them that power. Sometimes as children we unknowingly give them that power---as adults, we have to take it back.

We cannot give all of our lives to God if some of it belongs to the people in our past that have harmed us in some way. As a child I was violated by an authority figure I loved and trusted. This traumatic experience played a significant part of me becoming a ***'no'***. This experience triggered feelings of isolation, disconnect and shame. I felt responsible and felt it was my responsibility to atone for an event which was completely out of my control.

One of the first steps to recognizing our worth is realizing we don't have to prove our self-worth to anyone. Actually by giving up our need to control other's opinions of ourselves we find freedom in simply--- being.

Unlike our families, we don't have to prove our self-worth to our Heavenly Father. God offers us His unconditional love and needs no affirmation of our character. God accepts us just as we are. The apostle Paul tells us in 2 Corinthians 5:17: *"This means that anyone who belongs to Christ has become a new person. The old life is gone; a new life has begun!"*

My wife Linda often says “it is a million mile walk from your head to your heart”. Just because we know something intellectually doesn’t mean we believe it in our heart to be true. It seems that living out God’s teaching, isn’t always easy. Instead, we are driven by pride to produce evidence of how we have changed and how we are ‘new’. We forget that ‘actions speak louder than words’ and we attempt to explain each step of our journey to create an accurate depiction as to who we are at any given time. If you need to tell your family that you are a new person, then you may not be as new as you originally believed.

If we look at ourselves as a tree, the roots are important, but it is the trunk and branches that grow up from those roots that are seen by the world. So we have to remember that the roots of our journey may be our beginnings, but they do not have to dictate the future or be our destination.

***Proud people breed sad sorrows for themselves.* Emily Bronte**

5

PRIDE AND FRIENDS

For the sake of my family and friends, I will say, "May you have peace."
Psalm 122:8

Friends can bring out the chameleon in anyone. We bury any sense of our authentic selves or personal opinions to adapt to any particular social situation or discussion. As a '***no***', my need to be respected for my opinion, paled in comparison to my need to be liked.

That is what happened in my life. When I reached high school, I was determined to seek the approval from as many classmates as possible. I began this quest by hanging out with the student body's least judging clique—the potheads. I went from being unassuming to being the class clown, making every situation a performance to gain their approval. (Even now, I inject humor into a conversation to avoid appearing uninformed about the topic or simply to win people over. I am learning that it is alright to be silent and just listen).

Before long, I became a pot smoker too. Since no one has ever coined the phrase 'overachieving pothead', my soon-acquired lack of drive proved that phrase to be true. Since I was unable to impress my family, my prideful need for acceptance was focused on my peers.

I soon discovered the only thing that could make a person more popular than being a ‘funny pot head’ was becoming a ‘pseudo rock star’, so I joined a band. Our band’s world tour began and ended in countless parties thrown in the guitar player’s basement. The only exceptions were two performances at the Club Galaxy. Our first appearance there startled many of the club’s patrons. Just one night before, the Club Galaxy was an African-American “Gentlemen’s Club” and their customers were not made aware of its bold new direction. They were less than delighted to see the stripper pole replaced by four rock singers. The audience made their distain clear by throwing insults and plastic cups. Normally I would end up in the fetal position completely shutting down. The only thing that prevented a total retreat was my need for my band mates’ approval. Our return performance was drastically different, in that we realized the importance of inviting everyone we knew.

At our second show we received the ovations worthy of ‘rock stars’. As a ***‘no’*** I was totally enamored by the positive feedback from the audience. Being on stage fed my ego like a pride buffet. At that time I also partied like a ‘rock star, so my perspective was blurred by a combination of drugs and pride. As the pseudo front man of a rock band I was able to fool myself into believing that their accolades were both sincere and heartfelt. The world's approval may sometimes be sincere, but it is rarely unconditional.

It took me years to realize the world could never fill the void in my life. Despite my constant quest to be fulfilled I remained empty because I was unaware of what my life was missing. I found that being authentic was nearly impossible because I did not like myself. I discovered having a personal relationship with Jesus meant I didn't have to be 'funny' or be a 'pseudo rock star'. In fact, it meant I didn't have to pretend at all! I am a work in progress and even now I sometimes give into the temptation, to put on *a humble mask on my prideful face*.

Matthew 4:1 says: *Then Jesus was led out into the wilderness by the Holy Spirit to be tempted by the devil"* So I am not unique. Satan tries to tempt everyone--- even Jesus! This is further proof of our need for community. We need to be surrounded by fellow Christians to be reminded that we are not alone in this fight. Believing that Satan has singled us out or that our trials are more severe than others is just another form of pride. We read in I Corinthians 10:13: *"When you are tempted, God will show you a way out so that you will not give into it."*

Friends can either help lead us astray or help lead us to Christ. The key is to use the discernment necessary to choose the right friends. Unfortunately, we sometimes pride fully ignore or even replace friends whose advice we do not agree with. As a '***no***' when I would seek community outside of the church I would become 'actively isolated'. A person who is actively isolated refers to someone being surrounded by people--- but still feeling closed off and alone. I would have others to relate to--- without actually having to connect with them.

When I combined my tendency to be 'actively isolated' with my history of being the class clown, stand-up comedy was a logical career choice. Comedians are motivated by a distinct contradiction. We strive to relate to crowds to mask our inability to relate to individuals. It is because of this, that it is nearly impossible to nurture a sincere friendship with a fellow comic. In over twenty years in that vocation I have only had one—Chris, who has shared many adventures on the road, performing at what we lovingly refer to as "hell gigs".

The community of stand-up has three basic social classes: opener, middle and headliner. These social classes make most relationships in the comedy world very competitive. I can honestly say that in the two decades that I have performed on the road, I was never the headliner. This made me jealous on more than one occasion. The only feeling more spiritually damaging than having a prideful jealousy is deep-rooted resentment. I have heard my pastor describe this as drinking poison and expecting the other person to die.

In Galatians 6:4 Paul writes: *"Pay careful attention to your own work, for then you will get the satisfaction of a job well done, and you won't need to compare yourself to anyone else."*

I have always said that the easiest way to stumble and fall is by watching someone else's feet. The most unnecessary conflict is created by jealousy. My inner conflict was one-sided, and the other comedians were unaware of my feelings. Whether this meant the other comedians wrote better jokes, had a better stage presence or were willing to work harder to hone their craft---- their success was not intended to make me feel like a failure.

I believe resolving conflict always comes down to a combination of ownership and letting go. One of the few things both a '***no***" and a '***know***' have in common is an inability to own their portion of any conflict. Keep in mind that ownership does not indicate that one was right and the other was wrong. Ownership recognizes participation, and acknowledges that we have allowed the other person to cause distress in our life. We have to realize that there is freedom in letting go of the past.

During my stand-up comedian years I was the total embodiment of being a '***no***'. Performing stand-up lent itself to the '***no***' mindset in two specific ways. First, I could create a character that I could hide behind. Second, I could excel in self-deprecating humor by taking my negative inner dialog and simply adding a punch line. During my 'so-called' stand-up career I became the characters D.J. Fisher and Pudgy White. Neither of these people was really me.

Life on the road did not generate the best life style---so I drank, smoked and ate along with all of the other comics. Those poor choices actually helped to feed my biggest addiction at that time—laughter. The bar food and cold beers would bring on the pounds, and every pound would bring on one more "fat joke". In my heart I believed the audience was laughing at me and not with me so I found comfort in consuming even more food. I believe that's how sin works in general; we find comfort in a temporary fix and then annihilate ourselves over our human weakness, driving us back to our temporary fix again.

In many life decisions, we have two choices--- fight or flight. As we enter the battles of life, we do not need an army in front of us---but we do need a friend beside us. Friends are essential in helping us find balance and remain grounded.

- It's important to show respect for your friend's opinions and values, but not at the expense of losing self-respect.
- There is great value in friendship but friends are not a substitute for a personal relationship with God.
- A true friendship should be based on team-work, therefore no one should be building it alone.

As part of a comedic community that avoids authenticity like the plague, I could only share my pain with a roomful of strangers. It is like living in a prison cell with an open door. Although we are clearly free to leave, we choose to live in captivity because we find comfort in our emotional and spiritual shackles. Familiar pain is at least still familiar. Being on the outside of our prison cell can be as frightening as being inside it. And my so-called friends on the road were no help; they were in their own prison cell as well. God showed me I could leave my self-imposed prison cell, and find freedom in Him.

Life outside the self-imposed prison cell helps us to develop discernment when it comes to choosing our friends. The enemy will pretend it's our friend and tell us what we want to hear. The enemy will put friends in our lives that will help keep us trapped in sin. They will discourage us from making significant changes in our lives. My wife often says that, "We are always willing to make a change as long as the pain or inconvenience of the change isn't today." I can promise you the world if it requires effort in the future. Lifelong friendships do not happen in an instant. True friendship comes with growth, and true growth is developed over time.

***"The only thing in life that is instant are mashed potatoes… and they suck."* Linda Fisher**

6

PRIDE AND WORK

"Work with enthusiasm, as though you were working for the Lord rather than for people."
Ephesians 6:7

This is intentionally the shortest chapter in the book because in the workplace, even misplaced pride can have its rewards. It is almost impossible not to take on the same chameleon-type behavior that we display with friends into the workplace. This is because our employers have rules and guidelines that we all have to follow. That is what separates our jobs from all other aspects of our lives.

Actions, behaviors and relationships that are founded on pride, have a far different out-come at work. For example, trying to get along with coworkers is not only healthy but essential. Opinions that could start a debate among co-workers are usually best unexpressed. Harmony brings peace, peace helps us stay focused on our tasks, staying focused on our tasks increases our productivity and improving our productivity makes us better employees.

Paul tells us in Colossians 3:23-24: *"Work willingly at whatever you do, as though you were working for the Lord rather than for people. Remember that the Lord will give you an inheritance as your reward, and that the Master you are serving is Christ."*

The truth is that the office, factory or any work environment can push a multitude of 'pride buttons'. The first of, which is that stifling our personalities and opinions is encouraged and oftentimes mandatory. Our employers are not concerned with why we are going "above and beyond" as long we do. We are all flawed. We pale in comparison to God. This is by design because only God can fill the void in our life.

My work history is nothing, if not diversified. I have worked at an assortment of jobs and for an assortment of bosses with an assortment of dispositions. Since our work experience can be determined by the amount of feedback we receive, the relationship we have with our superior is crucial. In my lifetime, I have had good jobs and good bosses and horrible jobs and horrible bosses.

Karen was an excellent boss at an excellent job. She was very kind to me and when I needed a place to stay, she allowed me to find shelter in the back room of her business until I found an apartment. I was extremely proud to be Karen's favorite and most valued employee. I was responsible for writing all of the "specialty songs" for her singing telegram company. I was usually given the opportunity to wear something fun such as a tuxedo with tails or a gorilla suit, but not on Valentine's Day. On that day, I dressed as cupid with wings, red leotards, a bow and arrow and of course a diaper covered in hearts. On one Valentine's Day, I was on my way to deliver a telegram when I discovered I was lost, so I stopped and asked for directions. I did not realize until I stepped through the door that I was walking into a biker bar. I was thinking that I was about to become a human piñata. That is when I utilized my quick wit and told them if anyone made one false move I would put their eye out with my bow and arrow. After that they all wanted to buy me a beer.

A '***know***' might suppose that parading about in a cupid costume would be quite a humiliating event. But a '***no***' understands that assumption would be drastically incorrect. We believe in the concept of "whatever it takes" to get someone's attention and approval. Our pride does not come from the execution but the outcome. Even if the execution means being in a biker bar wearing a diaper.

At the other end of the spectrum would be Phil---- A horrible boss and a horrible job at national video store. Phil was in charge of the scheduling and repeatedly scheduled me for <u>every</u> major holiday. Phil, of course, did not work one holiday. Did I complain under my breath about how unfair he was while still working each and every holiday? Of course I did! Victims who constantly complain are filled with anger. Victims who suffer in silence are filled with pride. My issue with Phil was that as the assistant manager, I performed many of the same functions as he did for far less money and far less recognition.

As I continue to grow I am coming to the realization that this was not Phil's issue----but mine. At one point or another every '**no**' feels like a victim. It is easier for a victim to find fault and to blame others than to find self-awareness and healing. It is by God's grace I am learning that every step I take forward is by choice.

As a '**no**' I believed that everyone's position was more important and more significant than mine. As I continued to grow in my faith, I realized that there is nothing wrong with being extraordinary at ordinary things. I now understand that Phil could not excel at his job if I didn't excel at mine. Anytime we feel we are not receiving the recognition we deserve, we need to remember----God knows. God is well aware of our heart and our intentions and in His eyes we are all equal.

This is clearly illustrated in 1 Corinthians 12: 1-27: *"The human body has many parts, but the many parts make up one whole body. So it is with the body of Christ. Some of us are Jews, some are Gentiles, some are slaves, and some are free. But we have all been baptized into one body by one Spirit, and we all share the same Spirit. Yes, the body has many different parts, not just one part. If the foot says, "I am not a part of the body because I am not a hand," that does not make it any less a part of the body. And if the ear says, "I am not part of the body because I am not an eye," would that make it any less a part of the body? If the whole body were an eye, how would you hear? Or if your whole body were an ear, how would you smell anything? But our bodies have many parts, and God has put each part just where he wants it. How strange a body would be if it had only one part! Yes, there are many parts, but only one body. The eye can never say to the hand, "I don't need you." The head can't say to the feet, "I don't need you." In fact, some parts of the body that seem weakest and least important are actually the most necessary. And the parts we regard as less honorable are those we clothe with the greatest care. So we carefully protect those parts that should not be seen, while the more honorable parts do not require this special care. So God has put the body together such that extra honor and care are given to those parts that have less dignity. This makes for harmony among the members, so that all the members care for each other. If one part suffers, all the parts suffer with it, and if one part is honored, all the parts are glad. All of you together are Christ's body, and each of you is a part of it."*

In other words, everyone's job is valuable. No one is more important than anyone else because we all are working for God. Although Jesus is King, he worked as a humble carpenter. God does not want us to believe we are better than our workplace but to make our workplace better.

The only place success comes before work is in the dictionary. **Vince Lombardi**

7

PRIDE AND GOD

When pride comes, then comes disgrace, but with humility comes wisdom.
Proverbs 11:2

Many people believe that Satan's greatest weapon against Christianity is sin, but I believe that it is pride. Pride is completely about choice. We choose to be in control. We choose not to ask for help and we choose not to give God the power to govern our lives. As a '***no***', this behavior stemmed not only from needing my Heavenly Father, but also from needing Him so desperately that I believed I was beyond help. I came to the table feeling shame, anger, bitterness and jealousy. It is no coincidence that the more overwhelmed we are with darkness, the more we avoid the light.

In the days that Jesus walked the earth, tax collectors were one of the most despised people. They earned their living by cheating and stealing from the poor in their community. The darkness in which they lived was of their own choosing, so for many there was very little desire to break free.

In Matthew 9:9 Jesus encountered a tax collector that was unique from most others: *"As Jesus was going down the road, he saw Matthew sitting at his tax collection booth. "Come be my disciple," Jesus said to him. So Matthew got up and followed him."*

Two significant things happened in this scripture: Jesus approached a man that was considered despicable and asked him to follow Him. The other amazing thing was that Matthew, the tax collector, was instantly obedient. Jesus didn't say get your act together and I'll be back for you. He simply said, *"Come be my disciple."* We are no different. Jesus wants us just as we are. Never assume that God cannot use us because we are flawed. There are shadows in our lives where there should be light. God knows that the best way to draw flawed people to Him is to use flawed people as a guide. He meets us where we are, but He loves us too much to leave us there. Anytime you tell yourself, 'I can't do this,' you simply have not finished the sentence. What you need to say is, 'I can't do this… on my own.'

There are two other occasions where Jesus mentions a tax collector to illustrate our Heavenly Father's love and grace.

The first example is found in Luke 18:9-14: *"Then Jesus told this story to some who had great confidence in their own righteousness and scorned everyone else: "Two men went to the Temple to pray. One was a Pharisee, and the other was a despised tax collector. The Pharisee stood by himself and prayed this prayer: 'I thank you, God, that I am not a sinner like everyone else. For I don't cheat, I don't sin, and I don't commit adultery. I'm certainly not like that tax collector! I fast twice a week, and I give you a tenth of my income.' "But the tax collector stood at a distance and dared not even lift his eyes to heaven as he prayed. Instead, he beat his chest in sorrow, saying, 'O God, be merciful to me, for I am a sinner.' I tell you, this sinner, not the Pharisee, returned home justified before God. For those who exalt themselves will be humbled, and those who humble themselves will be exalted."*

For the purpose of this book, the Pharisee would be a '***know***' where the tax collector would be a '***no***'. As a '***know***', the Pharisee was very proud of his spiritual achievements. He expressed that by telling God how the tax collector paled in comparison. As a '***no***', the tax collector cried out to God still eclipsed by the shadows of his past. The tax collector recognized his need for God's love and acceptance where the Pharisee already assumed he had it. We cannot recognize if we already assume

The other scripture is Matthew 9:10-12: *"That night Matthew invited Jesus and his disciples to be his dinner guests, along with his fellow tax collectors and many other notorious sinners. The Pharisees were indignant. "Why does your teacher eat with such scum?" They asked his disciples. When he heard this, Jesus replied. "Healthy people don't need a doctor, sick people do."*

Jesus didn't wait for sinners to come to Him after they've been restored; He went to them while they were still broken. When I was a young naïve anarchist, one of my major misconceptions about Christians was that they were all robot-like conformists. The truth I later learned, is that they are quite the opposite. When we read the Gospel, it takes very little time to see that Jesus was a radical. He called the leaders of His day hypocrites and challenged their authority daily. In my youth, I thought I was being a rebel but in reality I allowed the world to define me. God doesn't just want to choose us… God wants to use us! For that to happen, for us to truly work for Him, we have to give God power over our lives.

To give God complete control we first need to be authentic with Him about everything that we are struggling with in our lives. We cannot hide our prideful nature behind our prideful mask.

Genesis 3:8-13 reads: *"When the cool evening breezes were blowing, the man and his wife heard the Lord God walking about in the garden. So they hid from the Lord God among the trees. Then the Lord God called to the man, "Where are you?" He replied, "I heard you walking in the garden, so I hid. I was afraid because I was naked." "Who told you that you were naked?" the Lord God asked. "Have you eaten from the tree whose fruit I commanded you not to eat?" The man replied, "It was the woman you gave me who gave me the fruit, and I ate it." Then the Lord God asked the woman, "What have you done?" "The serpent deceived me," she replied. "That's why I ate it."*

There are many types of behaviors to observe in those few sentences. The first behavior is that their initial reaction when they brought sin into the world was to hide. We also foolishly hide from God when we are in the grasp of sin. Of course we do not conceal ourselves behind a bush, but we do skip church that week, or neglect praying or reading His Word. We somehow believe that if we ignore God He will simply walk away. The other event that occurred in the garden was that Adam immediately blamed Eve. Shifting responsibility is as old as time.

Pride can be extremely immobilizing because we are so invested in how we will appear, that we believe that the best way to prevent failure is not to try. However, that is not God's plan for us. His plan is that we serve Him. There is a reason that God's plan sounds completely submissive. Serving Him not only teaches us to trust His divine power and wisdom, but also to trust the gifts and skills He has given us. Matthew 16:24 reads: "*Then Jesus said to his disciples, 'If anyone of you wants to be my follower, you must turn from your selfish ways, take up your cross and follow me.'*"

How can we pick up our cross and follow Jesus if we do not first put down our pride. How can we change the world if we are unwilling to change ourselves? I was first reminded of this ten years ago. It was the very first day I attended church with Linda. To be completely honest, I originally thought the message of changing the world was a sham. In Romans 15:6 states: *"With one mind and one voice you may glorify God and through God you can change the world!"*

We do not merely have the ability to change the world; it is why we are created. How can we look at our self-inflicted wounds and ask where is God? If we truly believe that our Heavenly Father is living within us, the real question is where are we? If we can focus on improving one community, one family or even just one life, we are helping to change the world. We can also teach the world!

When I was growing up, I was constantly told I was a failure--- so most of my life I believed that to be true. I now know that is a lie, and can now teach people about truth. Not with books and a blackboard, but with God's words and with deeds. We all have a lesson to teach because we all have a story to share. "My life looked like this but because I have a relationship with Jesus Christ it now looks like this." We are all wonderfully created and we all have an amazing story to use for a greater good.

Whether it is a painting or a sculpture, a film or a song, a masterpiece takes time. That includes us. It never just happens. God has a purpose and a plan for each of us and it starts by us recognizing that His great work has already begun. He is creating our lives to be the masterpieces that He intended them to be before we were even born. That is how God creates us into someone beautiful. Ephesians 2:10 states, *"For we are God's masterpiece. He has created us anew in Christ Jesus, so that we do the good things he planned for us long ago."*

Read the next section out loud. Meditate on the meaning of the words and allow the truth to move from your head to your heart. We are all on this journey and we are "works in progress". We will never be perfect. Let's stop having unrealistic expectations of ourselves---- and others. Let's show grace to ourselves and to one another just as Jesus did:

- I've allowed my pride to control my actions... but God isn't finished with me yet.
- I've been lost... but I've have found a new identity in Christ.
- I've made mistakes... but I am forgiven.
- I've made bad choices... but I am learning by the power of the Holy Spirit to make more honest and wise decisions.
- I've tried to live my life my way... but I have found peace as I surrender to a new way-----His way.
- I'm not perfect... But Jesus is, so I don't have to be.

God loves us. He sees us as someone who is kind, gentle and patient. We are all works in progress; We are never done learning, growing or changing because----God's not done with us yet. There is only one thing that is keeping God from completing His work in us---- and that is us.

We can be like a fresh mound of clay, flexible and able to be shaped and molded, or we can be like an old mound of clay, hard and impossible to shape and mold. There's so much more we need to discover and even more importantly, there is so much more God wants to reveal to us. So let's lay our pride at the cross, step aside and allow Him to finish His work in us.

It is my hope that this book sparked a desire to think about pride within your own life. I pray it starts us on a journey of self-enlightenment and change. We have learned that our past responses were the prideful byproducts of listening to the lies that the world told us. We have learned we are enough, not based on our deeds, but simply because God says we are enough. His love is unconditional and prideful behavior is an unnecessary obstacle between us and His love. Therefore, we no longer have to be a ***'know'*** or a ***'no'***, but we can be a ***'new'***.

Romans 12:2 says, "*Don't copy the behavior and customs of this world, but let God transform you into a new person by changing the way you think. Then you will learn to know God's will for you, which is good and pleasing and perfect.*"

There is nothing noble in being superior to your fellow man; true nobility is being superior to your former self.
Ernest Hemingway

8

ADDENDUM

Writing this book has been extremely healing for me. I believe this is because sharing my life in words has forced me to be completely honest. In the past few chapters I have shared stories that gave you a glimpse as to who I am and how I got here—these are a few more. Funny isn't always a mask or a defense mechanism. Sometimes funny is simply funny—and these stories are funny. Please keep in mind that all of these stories are slightly embellished but completely true.

♥

My brother was around the age of five when he first discovered fire. It was an early Saturday morning when he sat in the backyard lighting 'carbon snakes' with matches. It was particularly windy that day so my brother searched for the proper shelter for playing with matches. Unfortunately, underneath my bed is where my brother had decided was the second best place to play with matches—which also happened to where I kept my extensive library of Archie comic books. The obvious worst case scenario occurred; he set my comic books on fire, which became the perfect kindling to set my bed on fire. Normally I would not want him to set my bed on fire, however I was asleep in it at the time and could not form an opinion.

The moment I opened my eyes and saw the smoke I assumed I was in a dream sequence like on television. It wasn't until I began choking that I realized my bed was on fire. I jumped up and yelled, "My bed is on fire!" (Which I believe is the proper reaction when one's bed is on fire.) My mother snapped into action and ran in the room with glass of water. I informed her that my bed was on fire—not thirsty.

My brother called 911 and soon there was a fire truck and a crowd of spectators in front of my house. Never to be one to pass up an opportunity to entertain the troops, I felt like this would be an opportune time to put on a puppet show in the front window using my tube socks. My house was surrounded with policemen, firemen and concerned neighbors. Some of them putting out the fire, and some of them enjoying the puppet show---But I'm sure all of them were thinking, 'why is that odd chubby kid putting on a puppet show in the front window?'

Later that day I received an epic spanking because my father said, "All of those comic books are a fire hazard!" I responded, "They're only a fire hazard if someone is lighting them on fire, Dad!"

♥

For over twenty years I have spent the month of December playing Santa Claus. However, once I married Linda in 2003, playing Santa took on a whole new meaning. Linda and I had only been married three days before we spent our first Christmas together. I had told her I played Santa Claus, but at the time she just looked at me blankly as if to say 'ok, well that's a little odd'.

As we left the church service on Christmas Eve, I said, "I have to change into my Santa suit". Again, she seemed to respond as though the whole Santa thing was just something I considered but wouldn't actually do. But luck would have it we were only three days in and as we all know we are still on our very best behavior and willing to do anything to make our spouse happy----even if it is letting them play Santa. So reluctantly she helped me find a place to change.

We were early for my first visit so we decided to make a quick stop at McDonalds. Now this is odd because Santa is magical and therefore doesn't eat or drink, poop or pee. But anyone who knows Mrs. Claus knows it wouldn't be long before she would need a coffee fix. As Santa entered the restaurant everyone's eyes lit up and Santa entertained both employees and patrons. It was great fun, and the moment was filled with laughter and joy. She looked on in amazement as I told them about the rules of Christmas Eve, and how my sleigh is really a Ford Focus and those silly reindeer games are really hockey.

It was at McDonalds Linda discovered that when I put on the Santa suit something magical happens and I become Santa Claus. When we left, Linda was so excited; she immediately began to ponder who we would visit next. Many ask if Linda is Mrs. Claus. Well she will not wear the suit, but if you ask her she will say "I am the keeper of the schedule, I drive the sleigh and I fluff the suit". That was the beginning of the tradition and we continue each year to find great joy in playing Santa during the Christmas season.

♥

I have never killed, unless you count the cow. My mother and father went out of town for two weeks leaving their teenage son in charge of the family cow. I gave the cow lots of water and lots of food, and then I went off partying with my friends the entire time they were gone. I never saw the cow again until after his untimely demise. Unfortunately, my discovery came just hours before my parents were to return home.

The first thing that I had attempted was to prop the cow up in hopes that my father wouldn't notice. Okay, it wasn't the smartest idea but need I remind you--I was a teenager and I really didn't have too many options. I'm sure you have heard the expression 'dead weight', try lifting a deceased bovine!

Obviously this was an exercise in futility and I was never a fan of exercise. When my father saw the crime scene (because it's hard not to notice a dead cow) he truly handed out a punishment equal to the crime--a proper burial. Do you know how big a hole you have to dig to bury a cow? After many, many hours I dug a hole so deep I thought I could see people in China. I could swear I heard them say, "You idiot! You killed the cow!"

ABOUT THE AUTHOR

Daniel J. Fisher is a writer and performer with more than 20 years of experience. He has served in the youth ministry of his church as both a mentor and a speaker. Endearingly referred to as Mr. Dan, his passions have led to working with programs for children, including the Bradley Center and Boys and Girls Club of America. His mission is to help people grow closer to God and experience a more fulfilled spiritual life. As an example of Christ, Fisher wants to touch lives with his talents and inspire people to share their stories. He resides in Pittsburgh with Linda, his wife of 11 years.

FOR MORE TITLES FROM EX3 BOOKS

VISIT OUR WEBSITE AT:
www.EX3ent.com

Feel free to share your reviews of
A Humble Mask on a Prideful Face
via our website, email
ExpectedEndEntertainment@gmail.com, or
on Amazon.com.

www.ingramcontent.com/pod-product-compliance
Lightning Source LLC
LaVergne TN
LVHW051701080426
835511LV00017B/2659

* 9 7 8 0 9 8 8 5 5 4 5 2 8 *